Praise & Worship
HYMN SOLOS

15 Hymns Arranged for Solo Performance
by Stan Pethel

ISBN 0-7935-9685-8

HAL•LEONARD®
CORPORATION
7777 W. BLUEMOUND RD. P.O. BOX 13819 MILWAUKEE, WI 53213

Visit Hal Leonard on the internet at http://www.halleonard.com

2

BLESSED BE THE NAME ◆1

FLUTE

Traditional

O FOR A THOUSAND TONGUES TO SING
Text by CHARLES WESLEY
Music by CARL G. GLASER

BRETHREN, WE HAVE MET TO WORSHIP ◆2

Words and Music by
WILLIAM MOORE

FLUTE

COME CHRISTIANS JOIN TO SING ◆3

FLUTE

Words by CHRISTIAN HENRY BATEMAN
Traditional Melody

COME, THOU FOUNT OF EVERY BLESSING ◆4

Words by ROBERT ROBINSON
Traditional Music compiled by JOHN WYETH

FLUTE

FAIREST LORD JESUS

FLUTE

Words for stanza 4 by JOSEPH AUGUST SEISS
Silesian Folk Melody
Arranged by RICHARD STORRS WILLIS

HOLY, HOLY, HOLY ◆ 6

Text by REGINALD HEBER
Music by JOHN B. DYKES

FLUTE

I NEED THEE EVERY HOUR 7

FLUTE

Words by ANNIE S. HAWKS
Music by ROBERT LOWRY

I STAND AMAZED IN THE PRESENCE ◆8

Words and Music by
CHARLES H. GABRIEL

FLUTE

MY FAITH LOOKS UP TO THEE ◆❾

FLUTE

Words by RAY PALMER
Music by LOWELL MASON

O WORSHIP THE KING

Words by ROBERT GRANT
Based on Lyons,
Attributed to JOHANN MICHAEL HAYDN

FLUTE

PRAISE TO THE LORD, THE ALMIGHTY ◆11◆

Words by JOACHIM NEANDER
Music from Erneuerten Gesangbuch
Harmony by WILLIAM STERNDALE BENNETT

FLUTE

REJOICE YE PURE IN HEART 12

Words by EDWARD HAYES PLUMPTRE
Music by ARTHUR HENRY MESSITER

FLUTE

'TIS SO SWEET TO TRUST IN JESUS ◆13◆

Words by LOUISE M. R. STEAD
Music by WILLIAM J. KIRKPATRICK

FLUTE

TO GOD BE THE GLORY 🔶14

Words by FANNIE J. CROSBY
Music by WILLIAM H. DOANE

FLUTE

Majestically (♩ = 116)

WE HAVE HEARD THE JOYFUL SOUND 15

Words by PRISCILLA J. OWENS
Music by WILLIAM J. KIRKPATRICK

FLUTE